T0154213

The Flower Shop

charm, grace, beauty, tenderness

in a commercial context

Leonard Koren

Stone Bridge Press
Berkeley, California

The author wishes to thank the Blumenkraft staff, associates, friends, and customers for their many kindnesses during the preparation of this book. The author also wishes to thank Mikkel Aaland, Emilia Burchiellaro, Peter Goodman, Ron Meckler, Bill Tom, and Nan Weed for their advice and help during the book's construction.

contents

of
the
383
places
to
buy
flowers
in
Vienna,
why
Blumenkraft?

Extraordinary flower arrangements.
An inspirational environment.
Virtuous behavior.
Refuge . . .

The location. Blumenkraft is located on the ground floor of an ornate, late-19th-century apartment building in a Viennese neighborhood that combines a mild urban edginess with refined bourgeois comfort. Sharing the same block are four contemporary art galleries, three cafes, new and used clothing boutiques, a rare book seller, a champagne merchant, and an "upcycling" shop that sells lamps made of old bowling balls and other quirky recombinations of discarded objects.

cast of characters

Christine, Blumenkraft's founder and owner. 37 years old. Born and raised in a small village in Austria's Vorarlberg region, near the Swiss-German border.

Beginnings in the flower trade. As a child made long rows of flowers along the streets and lawns of her village. Two flowers, one stone, three leaves . . . And petals interspersed with stamens and stems—repeated over and over and over. At 13 she began working in a flower shop. At 15 she became an apprentice.

Vienna. At 26, she came to the big city "because of a man." She, the man, and the man's best friend quickly became famous in the city's bars and restaurants for their spirited behavior. But Christine didn't want to just hang out. She responded to an ad in a floral-trade magazine for a job in a new flower shop to be located at the epicenter of Vienna's big-spending flower clients, a block from the Opera House. Christine was hired, according to Peter, one of the shop's owners, because she seemed "very straight, very clear, and very centered." For the first two years Christine worked at Rosenkavalier all by herself, serving opera stars and other high-profile clients in-between preparing arrangements for parties and events.

The next step. She was happy at Rosenkavalier. She was paid well and learned a lot. It was like having her own business, she says. But Rosenkavalier was a fancy shop in a ritzy location, and this constrained her more creative impulses. For fun she made wilder flower arrangements for a friend's clothing boutique. She received lots of positive feedback. Some Rosenkavalier clients also began saying, "You're so good. Why are you working for someone else?"

Leap of faith. A storefront became available next to her friend's boutique. The friend urged Christine to take it. Right about then, Christine became good friends with Gregor, an architect. She asked him to look at the space. "Tomorrow we start?" he prodded. Other people were also interested in the storefront. Christine didn't have a financial—or any other kind of—plan but got a two-week option because the building manager liked her. He offered to make the rent especially low. . . . She signed a lease in May. Peter, her former Rosenkavalier boss, gave a congratulatory speech at Blumenkraft's opening party in December.

Qualities of a good florist (according to Christine).
• Solid, practical, arrangement-making technical skills.
• A good sense of humor.
• A distinctive sense of color and proportion.
• A deep feeling for human beings.

9

Andreas, the de-facto shop manager. 37 years old. Born and raised in a small village near Frankfurt, Germany.

Deciding to become a florist. At 15 he narrowed his career options down to social work or the flower trade. He chose flowers.

Early training. During his apprenticeship he was treated "like a dog." The shop's owner insisted that he work without gloves, even when handling flesh-piercing thorns, thistles, and spiky pine needles. "It will make you tough," she said. Andreas's hands were bloody for weeks at a time.

Advanced training. For his floral master's degree he attended the *Staatliche Fachschule für Blumenkunst Weihenstephan*, a small, naturalistically oriented school with a Rudolf Steinerian bent.

Detour from the flower trade #1. As an alternative to his compulsory two-year German military service, he worked at a facility for the mentally handicapped. He says it was "hard, funny, and satisfying" work and he considered doing it permanently when his service obligation was over. But there was a "dangerous downside": he became too emotionally involved with those under his care. "I liked them too much," he says. "I felt an unrealistic responsibility toward them." When his job ended, Andreas continued to go on vacations with his former charges.

Detour from the flower trade #2. He applied for admission to the Dusseldorf Art Academy, but his application was rejected. He was told that at 28, with a florist's education, his mind was "too fixed." Instead he went to Japan for two-and-a-half years to teach Western-style flower arranging. While in Tokyo and Fukuoka he also studied Ikebana and *kyudo*, the Japanese "way" of archery (which he continues practicing to this day).

Life as a florist. (Andreas's selective paraphrasing and partial translation of the poem "Das Blumenfest" by Hans Magnus Enzensberger.)

"I'm picking flowers.
I'm pulling flowers.
I'm ripping flowers.
I'm weaving flowers.
I'm binding flowers.
I'm inventing flowers.
I'm pulling flowers out of thin air.

"I charm with flowers.
I excite with flowers.
I seduce with flowers.
I wound with flowers.
I destroy with flowers.
I tenderly caress with flowers."

Wiebke, the de facto floral-decoration specialist. 37 years old. Born and raised in a small village near Stuttgart, Germany.

Earliest experience in the flower trade. At age 6 she sold etched chestnut leaves, river rocks, and wildflower bouquets at a stall she set up, with her older sister, along the street near their home.

Deciding to become a florist. "School was hell," so at 16 Wiebke decided to either work with animals, or with flowers. Swayed by her parents concerns that she would be doing "dirty, smelly, low-paying work in a zoo with coarse men," she began an apprenticeship in a flower shop. "I'm sure I made the right decision," she says.

Advanced education. She earned her floral master's degree at the *Staatliche Fachschule für Blumenkunst Weihenstephan*, the same school as Andreas (it's where they met). "It was a wonderful two-year period," she says. "My outlook on life and culture broadened and I connected with people of similar sensibilities."

Wanderlust. She yearned to live abroad. Her first choice was an English-speaking country, but she didn't think her language skills were good enough. The next best option was a German-speaking country with a different culture. She chose Austria over Switzerland.

Working in Austria. After moving to Vienna, she got a job at Rosenkavlier. After a few years she found the work boring. "I couldn't move forward creatively," she says. Christine, when she left to start Blumenkraft, asked Wiebke to join her.

Alexandra, the shop multitasker. 31 years old. Born and raised in a small village near Graz, Austria.

Education. She studied art history and communications at university. (She never formally trained as a florist.)

Decision to enter the flower trade. After university she worked at a prestigious Viennese public relations firm. After a particularly "shitty" day, she decided to quit. A few months earlier, her sister-in-law had showed her a magazine article featuring Blumenkraft. "It seemed like there was so much space there," says Alexandra. "Surely there could be space for me. I was naive. I didn't even know exactly what they did. But I wanted to find out." While still working at the public relations company, she asked Christine if she could work on Saturdays. Half a year later—after she'd tidily finished up all her obligations at the agency—she informed Christine she was available during the rest of the week also.

Parental dismay. In the region where she was raised, working in a flower shop means you sell flowers, period. Low status, low pay. When she told her parents she quit her "glamorous" job to become an apprentice in a flower shop, they were highly disappointed. "I'd always been the model daughter," she says. "I'd never rebelled. This was my chance."

Floral training. When Alexandra first came to Blumenkraft, she didn't want to make "mistakes." She thought they would expect something good from someone so "old." She had private lessons with each of the staff members. "It took a few months before my brain turned inside out," says Alexandra. "When I began to stop thinking so much I began to have fun."

Gregor, Blumenkraft's architect. 48 years old. Born and raised in a small village in Upper Austria.

Early architectural practice. Just out of architecture school, he didn't have an office. Instead he handed out business cards with the phone number and address of his favorite cafe. He sat there for six, seven hours a day, for almost two-and-a-half years, making drawings and conducting business. (The cafe was designed by Adolph Loos, the noted early-19th-century Viennese architect who wrote a famous essay equating architectural decoration with criminality.)

How Christine and Gregor got together. Christine fell in love with Gregor and realized that he should be Blumenkraft's architect. To win him over she came up with the idea of sending him violets every second or third day. (In the "language of flowers" violets symbolize secret love.) The violets arrived via taxis dispatched from different parts of town, so he wouldn't be able to guess the sender. After three months, Christine arranged a dinner party at her cousin's apartment. Gregor was the only guest she really wanted; the 17 others were just props. Everything went wrong that evening. Whenever Gregor was near, she couldn't complete an entire sentence. She fell out of her chair. And when Gregor helped her up, it just made her clumsiness worse. She accidentally pulled out the tablecloth and caused plates and silverware to fall on the floor. Guests asked, "What's wrong with you Christine?" When the party ended, she maneuvered Gregor and herself into the same taxi. En route she suggested stopping for a nightcap. In the bar she finally told him, "I'm Violet." Feeling totally humiliated she sank deep into her chair, onto the floor. Gregor, also deeply uncomfortable, followed her down. He turned the situation around, however, by taking her hand and kissing it, gently. They became boyfriend and girlfriend shortly thereafter.

The working relationship (according to Christine). Gregor never said, "Do you like marble, wood, metal . . . ?" Instead he asked Christine, "Do

you like Lenny Kravitz, Prince, James Brown?" He was able to translate her raw instincts into architectural reality. • Many of the physical details of Blumenkraft are based on Christine's idiosyncrasies, and on oblique poetic references. For example, the height of the metal shelves in the front room is based on the height of her hips. • Gregor was very good at sticking to the budget.

The working relationship (according to Gregor). "At our first meeting I was completely understood by her. She wanted pure creativity from me. It was the first experience I ever had of this. She enabled me to be free." • "Christine wanted us to grow something together: the first major reconceptualization of a flower shop in Vienna. We agreed it had to be new and it had to be fun. She has a very strong intuition whereas I have to think about things. But we were going absolutely in the same directions." • "I had no idea about flowers or flower shops. And I was so happy to find that nobody had really done a serious architecture of flower shops before. It was like discovering an entirely new architectural domain."

The extended aesthetic community. Others involved at Blumenkraft include Kamal (pictured) and Parakkrama, both from Sri Lanka. They come in early in the morning or late in the day and help with washing vases and processing flower and plant materials. There're also Christine's seven older brothers and sisters (Christine's the baby in the family). And cousins, nieces, and nephews. They constitute a flexible labor pool enlisted at particularly demanding times, like the Christmas season when the shop becomes a factory turning out wreathes and other decorations, or when a regular staffer is on vacation. Former staff members, like Viktoria, who went off to art school in London, also come back, from time to time, to work as needed.

shop design

The name. "Blumenkraft" is a conjunction of the words *blumen*—
"flower"—and *kraft*—"power." There are a few of ways of saying "power"
in German. *Kraft* describes a physical force like electricity—or a hammer
coming down hard on cold steel. It has nothing to do with the quaint 60's
English term "flower power," except in an ironic sense. "Blumenkraft" is
one of a new generation of smart, simple, elegant, multiple-meaning
German-language business names. It's an entirely new linguistic creation,
coined by Gregor. "The metaphoric power of flowers is based on a
paradox," he says. "They seem weak and fragile but they inspire visual,
emotional, and spiritual strength."

The place. When first leased, the space was divided into a warren of small, low rooms left over from the previous tenant, a home appliance dealer. During the remodel the partitions were removed and layers of wall covering were stripped away. Fluted cast-iron columns miraculously appeared. 350 square meters of open floor space and 7-meter-high ceilings were revealed. Christine characterized it as a revelation of "holy space." Gregor says the space was so "perfect" he didn't want to "violate it," so he attempted to keep the architectural modifications to a minimum.

Acoustics. All the hard surfaces—slate floor, plaster walls and ceiling, steel and concrete display furniture—bounce sound around crisply making the space very responsive to the moods of music, or any other sonic events.

Light. The space receives very little natural light—only in the front facing the street, and only for a few hours a day. To compensate, a quartz track-lighting system was set up along the perimeter walls. ("Track lighting is so tacky," says Gregor. "Someday, when we have a little money, we'll uplight instead.") Eight large hanging pendant lights were also installed. Their illumination radiates down in soft, sensuous shafts.

The worktable. The most conspicuous feature of the open-plan work-space is a nine-meter-long worktable. It's divided into three independent sections; there is no front or back so staff and customers can easily move across/through to either side. Each subsection is fabricated out of a single sheet of stainless steel that is gently bent into a large, hollow, fat-"T" shape. (The hollowness allows small children to crawl under and through—which they do.)

The table works well.
Stainless steel is an easy
surface to clean. Flowers
and other natural materials
contrast smartly with the
cool, hard, shiny metal.
There is one feature, however, that defies utilitarian
logic: at the slightest touch
of the hand or hip, the table
shimmies. Whether this
jello-like motion was
intended is unclear. This
much is known: Gregor's
drawings and model were
given to the metal fabricator. At some point during
the manufacturing process,
the fabricator realized that

the table would wiggle if knocked. He suggested cross-bracing. Gregor said no; it would compromise the "purity" of the hollow form. Immediately after installation, Christine tapped the table. An alarmed expression crossed her face. "It moves!" she exclaimed. The fabricator, standing nearby, was mortified. Gregor adroitly responded, "The universe moves." He then turned to a skeptical Christine and calmly suggested, "Don't worry. It will do some of the work for you."

The office. Off to the side of the open space is a cave-like opening in the wall. Contained therein is a laptop computer, fax machine, stacks of photographs and paintings leaning against the walls, piles of books, and a glass-topped table with two bullet holes. (The tabletop is an incomplete proto-type. In the final version Gregor wants to create a "bouquet of flowers" induced by the radial shatterings of nine projectiles.)

Photo murals. There are two photographs, one on each side of the shop. Gregor says they are part of the architecture. They "extend the space," "lengthen the view." The photographs change annually. They always deal with the topic of flowers, albeit in an abstract way. Two years ago it was a mattress covered with flower-patterned fabric. Last year it was two views of a motorcycle in repose, in a field of wild flowers and grass.

Display furniture: the pedestals. According to Gregor, the pedestals are metaphoric "flowers": high, solid-concrete "flower heads" resting on thin steel "stems."

Display furniture: the big rack. It has a "T"-shaped outline similar to that of the stainless-steel worktables; a tall structure in a tall space.

The flower hospice. A flower, during its stay at Blumenkraft, is typically moved two, three, sometimes four times into different provisional arrangements. During this moving from vase to vase—or during processing, or during deliveries to outside clients—a stem may break, or a flower's quality may become somehow compromised. In such cases the flower might be placed in the flower hospice. Hospice flowers are used as free giveaways to children and to friends of the staff, and for practice arrangements; Alexandra likes making bridesmaids' bouquets for her hypothetical wedding, and miniature flower bunches for Barbie dolls. . . .

Alexandra didn't want to see almost-perfectly good flowers thrown away. She felt "sorry" for them, so she took them home. Then she started expanding the flower hospice Christine began in the back of the shop, and became its "head nurse." "From a strictly commercial point of view, perhaps it's a waste of time to fuss with flowers you can't, or won't, sell," says Alexandra. "But since I'm not involved with the shop's management, I don't have to look at the 'big picture.' If I did, I'd probably throw the flowers into the recycle bin. Fortunately, I'm only concerned with the 'small picture.'"

toil

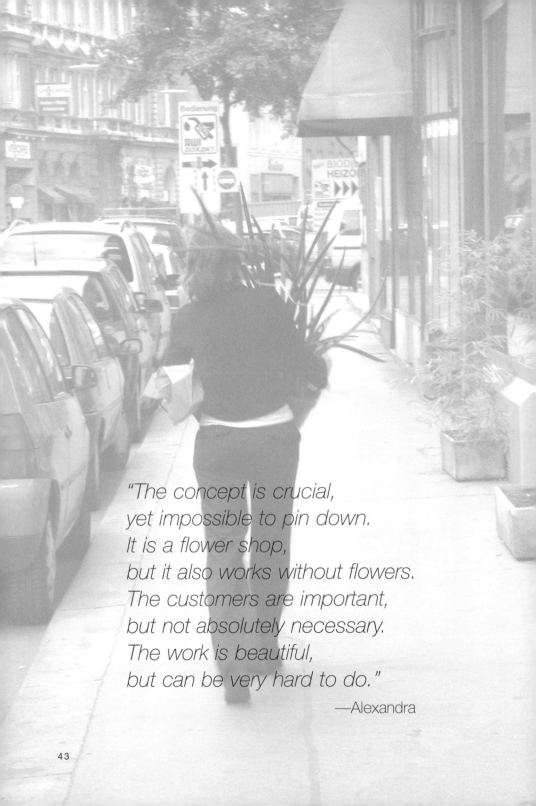

"The concept is crucial,
yet impossible to pin down.
It is a flower shop,
but it also works without flowers.
The customers are important,
but not absolutely necessary.
The work is beautiful,
but can be very hard to do."

—Alexandra

Ten-hour days are the norm,
9 a.m. to 7p.m.
Eleven-hour days—
8 a.m. to 7 p.m.—
are not uncommon.
And during the month and a half
leading up to Christmas,
80-to-90-hour weeks are typical.

"Seven weeks before Christmas, the Hard Times begin. They sneak into the shop and wait to ambush when the staff is most vulnerable. . . . The days become more than busy—so long and hard that you lose touch with whether your output is good or bad. But you have no choice but to go forward. Somehow you manage to keep a sense of humor and a grin on your face. But then comes the breakdown. Everyone desperately needs at least a few days off, but that's impossible. The cloud of positive feelings completely dissolves and the only thing left is work. I call this 'depression.'"   —Alexandra

"Sometimes when I go to arrange flowers for a wealthy client's dinner party, I'll see 20 bottles of the best Bordeaux on the table and think, 'I'd like to be able to do that.'" —Andreas

"Normally I'm not jealous that somebody has more money. Only when finances are very tight, when I can't pay suppliers, then I sometimes think, 'Am I doing this right?'" —Christine

aesthetic
and
methodological
inclinations

Every single flower. Everything that comes into Blumenkraft—every flower, plant, stalk, blade of grass—goes through the staff's hands. Stems of each flower are cut individually. Then they're treated so that the capillaries can draw water upward toward the flower head. Most stems are simply cut on the diagonal. Some are additionally cut, twice up the middle a few centimeters, into quarter sections. Woody stems require even more treatment. Lilacs, and all blossoming fruit-tree branches, for instance, require pounding with a hammer. Hydrangeas are run under hot or boiling water. And then some flowers—like lotuses and poppies—won't open by themselves once cut from the plant, so they have to be manually opened. . . . "Throughout all these processes," says Christine, "we look at *every flower* to find its unique, singular beauty."

Where Blumenkraft's flowers come from:

The public wholesale flower market, at the edge of town. Twice a week at four in the morning, one of the Bumenkraft staff makes the trek in the funny-looking shop truck. A stop is also made at a large, private, flower and plant wholesaler in the same area.

San Remo, on the Italian Riviera. They are delivered to Blumenkraft, in the middle of the night, wrapped in colorful Italian newspapers that the Blumenkraft staff neatly folds and reuses.

The traffic-stopping 14-wheel flower truck that makes a weekly trek from Aalsmeer Holland, site of the world's largest flower auction. Blumenkraft is stop number 35 on the truck's route through Germany and Austria.

From a wide variety of nontraditional suppliers, like Günter, a musician, performance artist, and landscape gardener. He rents a 2-acre field an hour north of Vienna where he grows things like hemp, heirloom roses, and wild berries. Whenever he sees something intriguing in the woods, or while on his job pruning exotic trees for wealthy clients, he brings the stalks, plants, or branches to Christine. "I'm interested to see what she'll make out of it," he says. "She never does the same thing twice."

Removing clutter. "Removing leaves from flower stems is like an ikebana practitioner bending things in an artificial way to make them appear natural," says Andreas. "Like an ikebana person might say, 'I'm helping a flower to achieve its natural expression.' If somebody buys 30 or 40 tulips, there's really nothing that needs to be done. The best we can do is to show the flowers as they are. But most of the time at Blumenkraft we have to choose between flowers and leaves. Between leaves and berries or fruit. Between leaves and stems. Leaves often compete with—obscure, distract from—the other stuff on the stems. . . . I would change nothing in a flower itself. Removing the leaves is merely giving the stem a haircut. Reducing but not destroying the essence. And the flower is the essence."

Modern vs. classic arrangements. Christine and the rest of the staff like "modern" arrangements more than "the classics." Classic arrangements tend to be symmetrical. They're either full, fluffy, or in a tight compact bunch. The colors are "harmonious." Classic arrangements are also interspersed with green things. Like a dense, roundish, bouquet of uniformly sized red roses, mixed with wisps of fern-like greenery. (At Blumenkraft these are called "rose bombs.") Modern arrangements, on the other hand, seem more naturalistic. They're more asymmetric and linear—either in the vertical or horizontal dimension. And the color combinations are much more heterogeneous. Modern arrangements are more "graphical," and a bit "out of proportion."

A delicate, surrealistic strangeness is the overriding quality of many of Blumenkraft's modern arrangements. This is primarily achieved by the use of three devices.

1. The combining of flowers that would never be found in nature together; flowers from different climatological, geographical, and/or geologic zones—say hyacinth, ranunculus, lilac, and anthurium—all together.

2. The use of long, narrow, malleable green lengths—*Equisetum hyemale* ("Dutch rush") or *Typhacea angustifolia* ("bulrush")—to physically tie all the elements of an arrangement together. Lengths of flat, thin *Typha* are woven back and forth, around and through the bottom of stems, like a snake winding it's way through a jungle. The same with the *Equisetum*, except it has articulated joints, like bamboo, so it crimps on twists and bends into hard-edged linear segments. Both grasses give the lower parts of arrangements the visual integrity of a bird's nest designed by Picasso.

3. The removal of all, or almost all, leaves from stems.

Transparency. "Cut flowers are abstract entities," says Andreas. "But you can push the level of abstraction much further if you arrange in glass so you can see the stems." One of the clear glass containers used most by Blumenkraft is not a vase per se; it's an aquarium. Christine brought one into the shop one day and liked the way it turned flower arranging into sculpture-like three-dimensional design. The proportions of off-the-shelf aquariums weren't to her liking though. So thumbing through the telephone directory she found a tropical fish dealer who could have them made to her specifications. Currently Blumenkraft stocks aquariums—renamed "blumariums" after a staff brainstorming session—in 18 different standard sizes and shapes. Blumariums solve many design problems: they can be invisible; their character changes completely depending on what you put inside; you can use them wet or dry; they're good for things big, small, monolithic, or in pieces.

Translucence. The stems of Blumenkraft arrangements are tied with a strand of raphia—a palm tree fiber—then the totality is wrapped in diaphanous white, waxed, vellum—a special paper used by traditional hat makers. The vellum is then crimped and stapled at one end, tied with raphia at the other.

Improvisation: using the circumstances of chance. "Two years ago," recounts Andreas, "Jutta, one of my closest friends, got married in an old castle in Germany. I arrived three or four days before to help with the food preparation—and to swim and take long walks. In the woods one day, Jutta asked if I would make her bridal bouquet. Our sensibilities are very related so I couldn't just make a banal classic round bouquet. Nor could I make a self-conscious modern one either. I came up with the idea of creating a performance. I went into the garden and wrote down some words on a piece of paper—a minimalist poem. An hour before the wedding ceremony I asked two friends, Barbara and Waltraud, to come to a big special room, along with Jutta and her fiancé. I placed Waltraud and Barbara in a triangulated position relative to me. I sat Jutta and her husband-to-be in chairs—like a king and a queen—with a view of the proceedings. Barbara slowly read the words I wrote. With each spoken word, Waltraud threw a single flower into the air, which I caught before it hit the ground. After all the flowers were thrown, I tied them—in the same exact arrangement as I caught them—with raffia. It looked random. Not stylish. Not contrived. But memorable."

Change. Twice a week the layout of display pedestals, blumariums, and vases—the interior design of the shop—is radically changed. Christine comes in and does it on Sunday afternoons and Thursday nights, helped by Kamal and Parakkrama. The entire shop gets stripped down and turned inside out. All the vases and blumariums are brought to the back and washed. Some are retired, new ones brought out. The largest blumariums are repositioned. Pedestals are grouped into new configurations. Flowers and plant materials are rearranged. The purpose of all this activity, according to Christine, is to "reanimate the spirit of the place." Also because it's "fun" to experiment with new kinds of flower containers.

How the shop's aesthetic order is created and maintained. Imagine the Blumenkraft concept as if it were a building, suggests Alexandra.

- The basement is the Blumenkraft concept—in its complex and indescribable entirety.
- The first floor is the shop's architectural design.
- The second floor is the arrangement of the display modules: the pedestals, the concrete benches, and so on.
- The third floor is the vases and blumariums that are positioned on the various kinds of display modules.
- The fourth floor is the flowers arranged within the vases and blumariums.

"You can disrupt the flowers—or remove them—and there will still be an order," says Alexandra. "You can remove the vases or blumariums, yet there will still be an order. You can disrupt the positions of the display modules, but there will still be an order. . . . And so on."

customer relations

The company culture. "Christine allows the shop to be unserious," says Alexandra, "and allows those of us who work in the shop to be unserious. We're allowed to drink a glass of champagne in the afternoon if we want to. We're allowed to turn up the music loud if we want to. We're allowed to make silly things out of flowers if we want to. None of these things are part of a strategy to attract new clients. But if a potential customer steps in while these things are going on and—by some strange coincidence—he or she likes these things too, then communication happens."

Peter, a regular customer, and his dog Paul . . . An aria—the birdlike trills of two angels—issues loud over the sound system. Intense, joyous religiosity permeates the shop. The structure of beauty is manifest; God is palpable.

Oskar's mother drops him off at the shop while she runs errands in the neighborhood . . . "I'm totally clear that a good atmosphere—relaxed, not highly structured—is an important part of the business," says Christine. "I want our customers to feel absolutely comfortable."

Miscellaneous occurrences on a Thursday afternoon.

• A little girl with Botticelli-like curls, dressed in all pink, glides in on a shiny silver scooter, accompanied by her nanny, similarly transported. "I'd like to buy some flowers for my mommy," she says. She opens her hand, "This is how much money I have." It's less than a euro. Christine smiles, ties up some orchids, wraps them, and takes the coins.

• A disheveled man in his late 20s orders 37 roses. Ten seconds later, "On second thought, make that 39." Wiebke surmises that it's the number of days since meeting his new love.

• Alexandra removes the petals off of some old roses, then wraps them up nicely. Twenty minutes later someone from the Das Triest, a boutique-designer hotel around the block, comes in to fetch the package. "It's a tiny favor we do for them," says Alexandra. "They put the petals into every toilet bowl."

• A sad-looking man shuffles in and orders a bouquet from Andreas. The message on the card accompanying the flowers reads: "The one who is lucky is feeling. The one who is unlucky is thinking."

• A fashionably dressed woman walks in and says she bought two dozen "chocolate cosmos" a month and a half ago. They wilted prematurely and she's angry, though not overtly. No receipt, no returned goods, but she wants compensation. Wiebke, smiling, whips up an arrangement. The woman leaves smiling too.

• Christine leaves the shop to do some pro bono work at the Kunsthaus, one of the city's major art venues. She will create flower arrangements for a Hell Fire Dining Club dinner to be held later this evening. The Dadaist-inspired meal, prepared by one of Vienna's finest chefs, will include "sick pig," "goose bacon," and "bat meat."

Customers like to deal with those they feel deserve their respect.
In other words, customers feel most comfortable interacting with staff
members whom they perceive as equals. Wiebke has charted it as a
hierarchy of staff qualities that Blumenkraft clients most esteem:

highest	• the ability to discuss the emotional aspects of flowers
	• the ability to discuss aesthetics
higher	• a wide-ranging, general cultural knowledge
	• being a creative person
high	• cleanliness; clean hands, nails, and clothes

Compassionate civility. "I like seeing customers to the door, same as when guests leave my home," says Wiebke. "It's a nice gesture of human concern. If I just walk away from the cash register right after the transaction, the customer might feel a slight emptiness. . . ."

Dealing with incivility. It is not difficult to imagine St. Valentine's Day as the perfect flower shop "moment": a glorious convergence of love and flowers at a temple of beauty. At Blumenkraft not a hackneyed heart shape is to be found—except for those naturally formed by tulip petals. Nor are there any Valentine's cards, or other obvious holiday commercializations; Blumenkraft is too sophisticated for that kind of stuff. Nevertheless, something is amiss. The shop's aesthetic sharpness is slightly off. There are premade bouquets—lessor versions of the normal Blumenkraft made-to-order-while-you-wait arrangements. And the music filling the aural space is neither soulful, inspiring, nor edgy. It's "Twenty Easy Listening Classics: Burt Bacharach," played over and over and over again. The shop is in a kitsch-by-default mode.

Then there is the clientele: considerably less refined than the usual, and not on their best behavior either. In fact, the mood is downright raw. It snowed the day before, snarling traffic, delaying obligatory Valentine's Day purchases to the last possible moment. Throngs of aggressive, entitled shoppers—"I want my flowers now!"—milling about impatiently. When it's their turn, most customers request unimaginative, clichéd arrangements: big, gaudy, lots of roses. The staff, keenly aware of the situation, tries to respond courteously. Nevertheless the speed and frenzy of the scene is inexorably draining humanity out of transactions. "They aren't our regular clients." says Wiebke. "People are unkind. They ask for things we don't have. And now we're running out of flowers."

. . . Two and a half hours after the shop's posted closing time, the last customer of the day brings the three remaining anthuriums to the work-table. He asks Andreas to bind them with *Typhaceae* grass in a character-istic Blumenkraft manner. Andreas politely says, "I'm very sorry but we're completely out of *Typhaceae*."

"BUT I WANT THE GRASS!" demands the customer.

"BUT WE DON'T HAVE THE GRASS!" Andreas replies in a harsh tone.

The man becomes docile and meek like a child.

"He's an idiot," Andreas mutters under his breath as he shuts the door on the worst day of the year.

making arrangements

"Sometimes a customer orders an arrangement over the phone and later calls back to say the flowers have arrived—but they're ugly. I politely tell them, 'There are no ugly flowers. Flowers are beautiful. What you probably mean to say is that you don't like the way we arranged them.'"

—Christine

"I decide which flowers or plants are good for a particular person. My calculation is based on their expression of need, plus an assessment of their character, their body language, the way they're dressed. . . . I also look around at the flowers in the shop and determine which is the most beautiful for me at that moment. It's also important for me to observe the person, to see their reactions as I pick flowers and arrange them under their scrutiny. I suspect they like that I'm carefully deciding which flowers are best for them. They're curious which I will choose. What unique solution I will come up with, for them only."

—Christine

"Sometimes clients ask, 'Is this a horrible flower selection for an arrangement?' I'll say, 'Not if you like it.' If someone is selecting flowers and plant materials I've never arranged together before—because in my personal aesthetic view they don't go together—there are two different ways I handle it. I either tell them that the elements don't go together. Or, I'll try to arrange it and let it be a new floral manifestation—one that I would never have reached without this particular client. Perhaps it's a little like eating sausages with strawberries. They don't go together exactly, but they don't taste that ugly either. So why not?"   —Alexandra

"When someone comes to Blumenkraft for the first time, it's like going into any other flower shop. When they come a second time, however, a game—a playful dialogue—begins. The specifics of the game change from client to client, from staff member to staff member. With most of our customers we're playing games— there's a story and a history between us. That's why working here is never boring . . . I never talk to clients about this game, but they know the rules."

—Alexandra

"When we arrange flowers, we're transforming their context. Although this 'bringing to a new context' can be perceived as 'art'—particularly in a Warholian sense—I prefer a more down-to-earth description: we're preparing flowers for sale."

—Alexandra

final arrangements

"Two or three weeks ago a woman came in and asked for an arrangement over a coffin. She was here for over an hour. We discussed her thoughts and feelings regarding the lost person. In a way it was kind of a performance. We started at one corner of the shop and walked around slowly. She said this person was very nice, simple, and strong. So I picked some thyme which has this simple-strong quality. It's also a symbol of cleansing. Then she asked for something to

symbolize blood. So we selected a branch of a Cornus alba sibirica *bush that becomes reddish in the winter. And then we picked white lily, a symbol of purity. And then blue hyacinths, the color of yearning for a primordial or mystical state—with bulbs attached so that the funeral guests could take them home and plant them in their gardens to renew the memory of the person every year. After our selections the woman said, 'I have to thank you. I feel much better now.'"* —Andreas

"A few months ago a man came in and said 'I have a question so please don't kill me.' I told him I don't usually kill my customers. He asked if I would come with him to the cemetery to do flowers together. I said yes, of course. He said he was very happy because it had been weeks since his 20-something artist girlfriend died—under mysterious circumstances—and I was the first florist who said they would help.

"Funeral ceremonies are generally so strict in form because of government regulations. The man wanted to change various things. He wanted the final ceremony at graveside, not in the chapel. I helped arrange this. He wanted a wreath with banners with last goodbyes written on it. He asked if what he wanted to write was too childish. I encouraged him. The arrangement on top of the coffin, the sheet of flowers, was also very important to him. It was like putting a blanket over a child so it doesn't get cold. A tender meaning.

"This grieving man needed the appropriate expression of his sadness. He needed to solve his sorrow. He needed to make this one last gift to his beloved. He had my personal mobile phone number. He called late at night. He became very dependent on me to keep the various funeral-related tasks moving along. But I didn't mind."

—Andreas